With the Compliments of

EXTERNAL PUBLICITY WING
MINISTRY OF FOREIGN AFFAIRS
GOVERNMENT OF THE PEOPLE'S REPUBLIC OF BANGLADESH

BANGLADESH

MOSAIC IN GREEN

BANGLADESH MOSAIC IN GREEN

Second Edition
March 2004

Chief Editor
Shamsher M. Chowdhury, BB

Editor
Zahirul Haque

Associate Editors
Salahuddin Akbar, Helal Uddin Ahmed
Muhammad Mustafa, Sheikh Mohammad Billal Hossain

Published by
External Publicity Wing
Ministry of Foreign Affairs
Government of the People's Republic of Bangladesh

Cover : Bangladesh is a tapestry of colours. Her panorama changes with seasons vastly variegated in colours. Fertile fields in green haze, soothing and flaming flowers in captivating grace, running silvery rivers, array of charming trees interspersing in perfect harmony–are vistas of delight and peace where toil and sadness cease. Above all, the subtle curtain of her greenery remains all–pervasive, which spreads its shade all over making the land a mosaic in green.

Back cover : The sun sets softly behind the melting fields of gold in the evening hue

White *Shapla*, Water Lily–national flower of Bangladesh. The pink is another variety.

The flower bedecked Central *Shaheed Minar*, Language martyrs' monument in Dhaka city built in memory of the students and others killed during the historic language movement on 21 February,1952. The day is observed across the country with due solemnity. It marked the first sprouting of intense nationalist feeling of the people. Immortal 21 February (*Amar Ekushey*) is a landmark in the process of forging the country's cultural identity that triggered a heroic movement against attempts to stifle Bengali - the mother tongue of the people of Bangladesh. The day is now observed all over the world as International Mother Language Day as declared by the UNESCO.

National Martyrs' Memorial at Savar near Dhaka commemorating the supreme sacrifice of millions during the War of Independence in 1971

BANGLADESH
MOSAIC IN GREEN

EXTERNAL PUBLICITY WING
MINISTRY OF FOREIGN AFFAIRS
GOVERNMENT OF THE PEOPLE'S REPUBLIC OF BANGLADESH

CONTENTS

FOREWORD

This is a kaleidoscopic presentation of our land called Bangladesh, its valiant people imbued with a sense of history, its rich and varied flora and fauna, its verdant landscape with lush green fields, enchanting hills and hillocks and the meandering rivers falling into the vast blue expanse of the Bay of Bengal. It is a land of enormous economic potentials, inhabited by diligent and hard-working people who have a love for heritage. It is a land of ancient and variegated religious and cultural traditions. All of these together make Bangladesh a colourful mosaic of nature's splendour and bounty.

A proud nation, endlessly engaged in using its glorious past as a springboard for securing its rightful place in the comity of nations, Bangladeshis are currently working hard to improve their lot. I am convinced that due to the bold upsurge and their untiring efforts in nation building, Bangladeshis will soon be able to achieve their goal of a self-respecting nation by transforming their land into an abode of peace and prosperity for themselves.

Today, the world at large has been taking a renewed interest in the current resurgence of Bangladesh with its praiseworthy performance in economic growth as well as in strengthening democratic institutions. It has, therefore, become all the more necessary to present the country to the outside world in its true perspective. This book is a compilation and presentation of pictorial record of the true essence and perennial beauty of Bangladesh. I am confident that this edition of 'Bangladesh : Mosaic in Green' published by the External Publicity Wing of Ministry of Foreign Affairs will meet the needs of projecting the country and serve the purpose for which it has been designed.

KHALEDA ZIA
Prime Minister
Government of the People's Republic of Bangladesh

A reserve forest of *'Shaal'* trees alongside low-lying water body filled with water lilies

INTRODUCTION

Bangladesh has been described as a new state in an ancient land. Much has been written about the past glory of Bangladesh, notably in old records like the evidence of Pliny and Periplus of the Erythrean Sea (first century AD). It was drawn in Ptolemy's map. These indicate that from the earliest times Bangladesh was known to the West, particularly for its Muslin, the finest fabric the world has ever produced.

China Rose, known as *Joba*, widely blooms in Bangladesh

Travellers and scholars who were attracted by the charms and fame of Bangladesh since time immemorial had showered effusive epithets on its bounties and wealth, affluence and prosperity, craftsmanship and cultural advancement. They include the Chinese travellers–Fa-hien (fourth century AD), Hiuen-Tsang (seventh century), Ma-huan and Fei-shin (fifteenth century), Ibne Batuta (fourteenth century) from Africa, Nicola Kanti (fifteenth century) and Caesar the Frederik (sixteenth century) from Venice, Varthema, an Italian in the sixteenth century, Barbosa and Sebastian Manric (sixteenth century) from Portugal, Travernier and Bernier from France (seventeenth century) and Ambassador Ralf Fish (sixteenth century) of Queen Elizabeth- I.

To Ibne Batuta, Bangladesh was a 'hell full of bounties and wealthiest and cheapest land of the world'. So great were the attractions of Bangladesh that to quote Bernier 'it has a hundred gates open for entrance but not one for departure'. Ladies of Imperial Rome were literally crazy for Bangladesh's Muslin and luxury items, which according to Pliny, resulted in serious drain of gold of the Empire. Because of its location, Bangladesh served as a flourishing entry port and intermediary in trade and commerce between South Asia and the Far East. The region also played a seminal role in disseminating its belief, art and architecture in the wider world of Asia. Ancient Bangladesh took great pride as a coveted seat of learning and education and scholars from far away countries regularly flocked to its numerous universities and monasteries.

Etymologically, the word 'Bangladesh' is derived from the cognate *Vanga*, which was first mentioned in *Aitarey Aranyaka*, a Hindu scripture composed between 500 BC and 500 AD. Literally it means a wetland. Muslim merchants of Arab origin used to refer to it as *Bangalah* from which its present nomenclature is believed to have gradually evolved.

Geological evidence indicates that much of Bangladesh was formed between 1 to 6.5 million years ago during the tertiary era. Human habitation in this region, therefore, is likely to be very old with the evidence of paleolithic civilization dating back to about 1,00,000 years.

Bangladesh has an area of 1,47,570 sq. km and occupies the apex of the arch formed by the Bay of Bengal into which all the rivers flowing through the country drain. Bangladesh has one of the most complex river systems in the world numbering about 230 including tributaries having a total length of about 24,140 km. The climate of Bangladesh is characterised by high temperature and high humidity, heavy rainfall and seasonal variations. Daily temperature ranges from 10°C to 12°C in the cool months and in other months it varies between 28°C and 40°C. Soil of Bangladesh may be divided into three main categories, namely hill soils (Chittagong and Sylhet regions), terrace soils (Barind and Madhupur tracts) and alluvial and flood-plain soils.

Bangladesh contains greater bio-diversity than that of many countries taken together. Indeed few countries in the world can match its rich and varied flora and fauna, which are not only a unique biological phenomenon but are also a great natural resource of the country.

Bangladeshis are historically descendants of various races and nationalities. An Austro-Asian race first inhabited this region followed by Dravidians and Aryans. There was also an influx of the Mongolians from Tibet and Myanmar. The Arab Muslims started coming here in the early ninth century AD. Persians, Armenians, Turks, Afghans and lastly the Mughals followed in quick succession. Bangladesh has a population of 133.4 million with an average density of around 900 people per sq. km. It is the third largest Muslim country. Traditionally a land of communal harmony, followers of other religions enjoy full freedom of worship. The economy is mainly agrarian.

Doel, Oriental Magpie Robin, national bird of Bangladesh

16

Coconut, a household fruit in Bangladesh, abundantly grows in the southwest and coastal areas

Recently there has been a spurt in industrialisation with the utilisation of country's available natural resources and manpower. Trade and commerce are increasing and widening. Bangladesh is a repository of rich cultural heritage and tradition.

Long colonial exploitaiton has largely denuded Bangladesh of its past affluence and wealth. Independence, however, opened up new vistas of prospects and opportunities. In the final analysis, Bangladesh is a land of splendour and natural grace–a veritable mosaic in green, verdant and boisterous, with its dedicated and creative people adding colour and vibrancy to its being.

The Royal Bengal Tiger. Bangladesh boasts of being the abode of this world famous species of cat family, which enjoys the status of national animal of Bangladesh. Of dark yellow colour with black stripes, the Bengal Tiger that moves majestically is now a globally threatened species. According to a recent census, they total around 500 in their last stronghold in the southwest of the country - Sundarbans, world's largest mangrove forest.

17

Hanging nests of *Babui Pakhi*, Baya Weaver birds. This species of birds which weave their nests in summer are found across the country.

Below (left) : *Ghughu*, a spotted Dove, one of the variegated species of birds, noted for its sonorous call

Below (right) : Scaly-breasted *'Munia'* in a paddy field

A pair of Asian cuckoo.
Colour differs for male and
female. The black one is male.

A white male of Asian Paradise-Flycatcher, known in Bengali
as *'Rumal Chora Pakhi'*, meaning 'stealing a handkerchief'

A colourful *Machhranga*, Kingfisher.
These eye-catching birds live on fish
and swarm the country's innumerable
water bodies, lakes and rivers.

19

Top (left) : *Kamranga,* Star fruit, a sweet and sour fruit available throughout the year

Top (right) : Star Apple, *Jamrul,* a juicy summer fruit of the country

Kathal, Jackfruit, national fruit of Bangladesh

Top (left) : *Litchi*, a juicy and delicious fruit of summer

Top (right) : Mango ranks top among all fruits

Papaya, a tropical fruit, grows
abundantly in the country

21

A colourful leguminous flower known as *Aporajita*

Top (right) : Canna, known as *Kalaboti*, grows widely during summer and rainy seasons

Tiger Lily, an exotic flower, blooms in the rainy season

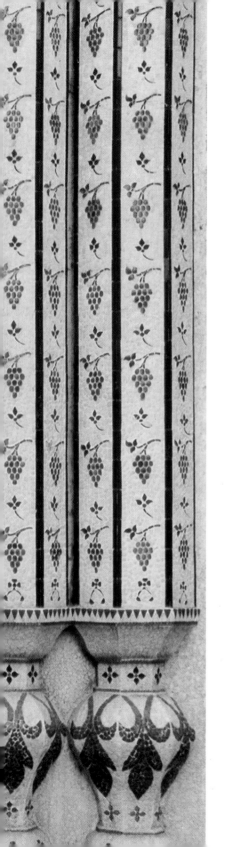

HERITAGE

Bangladeshis are a proud nation with a rich heritage. A heroic people, their long and turbulent history is replete with epic saga of their independent and indomitable spirit. In the ancient and mediaeval periods, Bangladesh's sway extended over a vast area including Sri Lanka, Maldives and Myanmar as well as Southeast Asia and the Far East. For nearly one thousand and five hundred years, this region played an important part in the great cultural fusion among the diverse civilizations of eastern and southeastern Asia and reached the zenith of economic affluence. Its fame as one of the most prosperous lands in the world spread far and wide.

The long chain of Buddhist and Hindu rule was broken by the advent of Muslims of Central Asian origin in the thirteenth century. A succession of Muslim monarchies ruled over the area till 1757, when the British conquest took place. The Muslim rule was the golden era in the annals of Bangladesh. After almost two centuries, the British left and Bangladesh formed the eastern wing of Pakistan.

Soon, the people realised that the new post-British arrangement was far short of their aspirations; their nationalist struggle took a new shape culminating in the War of Independence in 1971.

Facade of Kantaji Temple, built in 1752 in northern town of Dinajpur, one of the most ornate temples in Bangladesh

25

Ornated pillars along the veranda of an old house
of Sonargaon, the oldest capital of Bangladesh

Top (right) : Egarasindhu Mosque at Kishoreganj district. Remnants
of a 17th century dome-shaped mosque of pre-Mughal period.
Adjacent to the mosque is a two-segment (*do-chala*) building,
which resembles a hut, used as gateway to the mosque.

Devotees at a Buddhist Pagoda

The people of Bangladesh mounted one of the most effective guerilla wars of modern times on 26 March 1971. The nine-month long war, which cost countless lives, was the most glorious chapter in the history of Bangladesh. On December 16, 1971 the War came to an end, the people emerged victorious and after centuries of subjugation Bangladesh became an independent nation.

Inner view of *Shait-Gumbad Mosque*, built in 1459 at Bagerhat in southern region of Bangladesh. The prayer hall of the mosque has rows of arches that support the 60 domes of the imposing structure.

Barendra Museum at Rajshahi town in northwestern Bangladesh. The museum has a rich collection of ancient stone-made icons of Lord Buddha and many Hindu deities.

Exhibits of old terracotta preserved in Paharpur Museum of greater Rajshahi region

Saat Gambuj Masjid, a seven-domed mosque of Dhaka built during the Mughal rule in Bengal

Below : The 18th century Kantaji Temple constructed with bricks and terracotta

Dhakeswari Temple, one of the oldest Hindu temples in Dhaka city, is a leading place of congregation during Hindu religious festivals

Baitul Mukarram Mosque, the national mosque in the centre of Dhaka city, was built in 1962. It resembles the structure of Holy Kaaba with a fine blending of modern architecture.

Top (left) : Sculpture on the Rajshahi University campus depicting armed freedom fighters of 1971 War of Independence

Top (right) : Architectural site of Paharpur Buddhist Monastery in the northern district of Noagaon. Built during the rule of the Pala dynasty, it was the largest seat of Buddhist learning in South Asia. The architecture of the pyramidal cruciform temple was largely influenced by those of Southeast Asia, especially Myanmar and Java of Indonesia.

The ruins of 7th century Buddhist Monastery at Mainamati, near Comilla district town. Large-scale excavations at Mainamati archaeological site have revealed valuable information regarding Buddhist rulers who flourished here as independent kings.

Historic scenes of valiant freedom fighters returning to Dhaka after the surrender of occupation forces on 16th December 1971. Bangladesh emerged victorious as an independent and sovereign nation on 16th December of 1971; the day is observed as Victory Day.

Below (left) : Zia Memorial Museum at Chittagong–homage of the nation to a valiant freedom fighter who had proclaimed the country's independence

Below (right) : The Folklore Museum at Sonargaon, 27 km away from Dhaka city. For three hundred years from 10th century AD, Sonargaon was the capital of mediaeval Bengal. The Museum projects rich cultural heritage of Bangladesh.

The impressive Curzon Hall, named after British Viceroy of the subcontinent Lord Curzon, representing Victorian architectural form, now used as the Science Faculty Building of the University of Dhaka. It was built as the Legislative Assembly Building of Assam Bengal province in British India.

Shilaidaha Kuthibari - the historic bungalow of Nobel laureate poet Rabindranath Tagore. The poet used to visit this place frequently in connection with the administration of his Zamindari. The quiet resting place provided a needed atmosphere to devote his times to writing. The place is located 20 km away from the district town of Kushtia.

Below : Palace of Queen Bhawani, now known as *Uttara Ganabhaban* at Natore, 225 km to the north-west of Dhaka. Built nearly 300 years ago, Queen Bhawani's palace is reminiscent of its past glory and architectural value. The enchanting sight of the palace and its premises attract tourists from all over.

THE LAND

The landscape of Bangladesh is a tapestry of greenery. Across the tropic of cancer, it lies in the northeastern part of South Asia between latitudes 20° 34' and 26° 38' north and longitudes 88° 01' and 92° 41' east. The country is bordered by India on the west, north and northeast, Myanmar on the southeast and the Bay of Bengal on the south. Strategically located, Bangladesh is virtually a bridge between south and southeast Asia. It has a landmass of 1,47,570 sq. km criss-crossed by a network of several major rivers, their numerous tributaries and canals forming a lace of interconnecting channels. In fact, Bangladesh is the largest riverine delta in the world. The extensive river systems are fundamental to the country's economy and the people's way of life. Its low, flat, alluvial deltaic plains present an enchanting vista of vast verdant green fields sweeping across the horizon. Bangladesh has some of the world's most fertile agricultural lands accounting for abundant growth of various crops. The northeastern and southeastern parts of the country are dotted with small hills and ridges, their average elevations being 244 metres and 610 metres respectively. The highest peak *Keokradong* at the southeast end of Bandarban district rises 1,230 metres above the sea level. Thus with its variegated topographical features, Bangladesh appears like a vibrant motif splashed with enchanting beauty and serenity.

A mustard field in full bloom sprawling out into the horizon

Autumn is the harvesting season in Bangladesh when paddy is collected from the fields and threshed. Threshing is mostly done in traditional way by bullocks.

Below : Riding on buffaloes, a common scene in rural areas

Driving down the country across the horzion, they get a feeling that they should be there where they belong

The snow-white *'Kaash'* flower marks the advent of early Autumn

Teknaf, the southern-most tip of Bangladesh, well–known for its enchanting scenic beauty alongside the sparkling blue expanse of the Bay of Bengal

Left : A countryside scenery. Palm trees grow abundantly in Bangladesh.

Below : The rich alluvial and fertile land helps luxuriant growth of paddy and other crops like jute, wheat, sugarcane and tea

A cow-herd is returning home along the sea-beach at twilight

The sea-beach of Cox's Bazar–the world's largest unbroken stretch of golden sand against the vast expanse of blue water and white surfing waves

Clusters of *'Kaash'* flower along a river-side displaying a spectacular autumnal serenity

Below : A picturesque scene of the Kaptai lake with its emerald green water flowing along the hills in Chittagong Hill Tracts region. The 680 sq. km man-made lake was formed due to damming of the Karnaphuli river.

Top : A view of the Teknaf market in autumn before harvesting of paddy against the silhouette of distant high rising hills on the Myanmar side across the Naaf River

Below : In riverine Bangladesh, boats play a vital role in the lives and livelihood of the people. Fishing boats with colourful sails floating on a river.

A tribal village on the slope of the hills. Fifteen indigenous tribes live in Bangladesh in different parts of the country but majority of them live in the Hill districts of Rangamati, Bandarban and Khagrachhari.

Left : A bamboo bush stands against the vast expanse of full-blooming mustard field – a typical winter landscape of rural Bangladesh

Fishing boats in the Bay of Bengal along the coast of St. Martin's, the only coral island in the Bay. The tranquillity and enchantment of the island surrounded by the vast expanse of blue sea attracts tourists from all over.

Different varieties of nets are used for fishing in Bangladesh. The trap net is one, which is put under water and at intervals brought above to collect the catch.

45

A speeding train passing through a hilly area. Bangladesh railway operates a track of 2880 km and provides passenger and cargo services throughout the country.

Kuakata is an unspoilt sea-beach in the southern district of Patuakhali. Here, one can see both sunrise and sunset from the same place.

46

A fascinating view of the Chittagong Hill Tracts, surrounded by Karnaphuli, Sangu, Matamuhuri and Feni rivers and their tributaries

Snow-white clouds hover above the famous Kaptai lake flanked by hills and evergreen forests. The man-made lake was formed when a river-dam (153 feet high, 1800 feet long) was built for hydroelectric power.

Paddle steamer retains its old charm. In this competitive age of marine vessels, these steamers still attract travellers for a more relaxing and enjoyable journey.

Jamuna Multipurpose Bridge, 11th longest in the world, connects the east
of the country with the northwest. Constructed with financial assistance from
the Japanese government, the World Bank and the Asian Development Bank,
the bridge was opened to traffic in June 1998. About 4.8 km in length, 18.5 metres
in width and costing some 39.5 billion Taka, the bridge has provisions for railway,
gas pipeline, electricity transmission and telecommunication cables.

Flowers of silk cotton tree, locally known as *Shimul*, blooms in early summer. Besides adding colour to nature, it contributes to local consumption of cotton.

Below : Buffaloes graze in the field along an eroded river bank. Cattle rearing is a profitable enterprise in rural areas.

A village market under a huge Banyan tree.
People carry local produces to the market
by bullock and buffalo carts - a traditional
mode of transportation in remote areas.

A colourful contrast:
white geese in a pink lily pond

SEASONS

Bangladesh is a land of six seasons. Each is distinct from the other. With the change of each season, landscape changes its colour and charm. The changing faces of nature also moulds the minds of the people.

The Summer is characterised by sweltering heats punctuated at times by Nor'wester (locally called *Kalboishakhee*) with thunder, lightning and hailstorm. But summer also has a lingering appeal as it offers an array of sweet fruits.

Next comes the Rainy season with torrential downpours often flooding rivers and inundating meadows and countryside. The country bathes in fresh waters when exotic flowers bloom and the rhythm of rainfall plays a symphony.

Rainy season over, early Autumn appears sending soft and slivery clouds across the azure sky. When autumnal moonlight falls on swaying *Kaashphool* along riverbanks at night, it creates a romantic aura all over.

Late Autumn is known as the harvesting season. Ripe yellowing paddy fields with mists, fog and dew–drops on the petals of fragrant *Shiuli* flower adds a mystic look to the surrounding.

The Winter overlaps the late Autumn, when weather usually remains dry and temperature goes down considerably. It is also the season of variety, of vegetables and delicious country–cakes called *pitha*. Spring, *Writuraaj*–king of all seasons, rounds off the Bangla calendar. It is the season of music, merriment and festivals, blossoming flowers and singing birds, bees and butterflies.

Kadam, a native flower which is thought of as heralding the monsoon

Below : Cracks in a crop-field due to drought in the summer

53

Top (left) : In rainy season, some crop-fields and meadows often go under water. Yet the farmers go on ploughing for their next crop.

A walk in the rain

Shiuli flower blooms in autumn evening, evaporates fragrance throughout the night and then sheds out in the morning

Advent of early autumn. Soft and silvery clouds and clusters of white *Kaash* flowers sway in harmony against the blue sky.

Extraction of juice from date trees - a common sight in winter. The juice is used as drink, molasses and as ingredient for *Pithas*.

Fishing in a misty winter morning

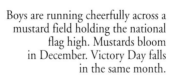

Boys are running cheerfully across a mustard field holding the national flag high. Mustards bloom in December. Victory Day falls in the same month.

In spring, trees assume a fresh
look with tender leaves and foliage

Palash, an indigenous
flower, blooms in spring

PEOPLE

Bangladeshis are simple in nature. Since time immemorial, they have been noted for their valour and resilience as well as hospitality and friendliness. Bangladeshis are also equally known for their creativity. They have an innate quality of open–mindedness. Communal or ethnic feeling is alien to them and despite diverse racial mix since ancient times, they are, by and large, a homogeneous group. Bangla is the common language of the people which holds official status and exalted position because of the richness of its literature. Fish, rice and lentil constitute the main diet of the masses–the vast majority of whom live in villages. A cotton *lungi* and a shirt are the common attire for men in rural areas. The urban people have largely adapted to Western costume. *Sari* is a common dress for women both in cities and countryside.

Bangladeshi women are traditionally adored for their charm, beauty and elegance. They are now increasingly adapting themselves to changing needs of time, working shoulder to shoulder with the menfolk in fields, factories and offices. In fact, they can be found in all professions and there is no exclusive male domain. Agriculture and its allied fields still provide the main livelihood of the people. The expanding industrial and service sectors together with trade and commerce offer increasing alternative occupations for the people.

There are about two million, mostly of Mongoloid origin, tribal people, the majority of whom live in the Hill Tracts districts. They zealously guard their customs, traditions and cultural heritage, which are quite distinct from one another and, till today, largely remain intact. For their living, they mainly depend on traditional cultivation called *jhum* and cottage craft, in which they greatly excel.

A happy village girl

Bangladesh has a tradition
of craftsmanship in clay pottery.
A girl is decorating a clay pot.

Right : Craftsman at work with *tabla*
(tabor)–traditional instrument played
in accompaniment with songs and music

Rewards of hard labour. An old farmer looks
at the bundle of golden paddy sheaves in his hand.

A hardy man tilling his land with the bullocks

Earthen ornaments is comparatively more popular among urban women. They are seen choosing their selection in a city fair.

Top (right) : Traditional way of spinning spindle for weaving cloth

A roving betel-leaf seller. Chewing betel-leaf with nut, lime and other aromatic spices is a common habit of many, especially the aged. Offering betel-leaf to guests is a traditional social custom.

A young woman in traditional costume at a spring festival

Tiny tots playing carom during a lesson break

A diamond polishing factory in the
Export Processing Zone. EPZs have
infrastructure facilities for foreign
investment in the country.

National flags are hoisted in observance of National Days. Flag vendors seen roaming on such occasion.

Top (right) : Jumping into river in groups is a fun in hot days of summer

Ha du du : A traditional and popular game in the rural areas

Farmers wear *Mathal* for protection against sun and rain while working in fields

A tribal woman weaving handloom cloth which bear characteristics of its own

Fishing in the Bay of Bengal,
which is rich in sea fish resources

Group fishing

Top (left) : Goat-rearing has become a profitable enterprise. Bangladesh exports black goat hide, which has a great demand abroad.

Top (right) : Drying paddy in sun in the courtyard of a house in rural Bangladesh

Women of *Santal* tribe working in a field. The *Santals* mainly live in the northern region of the country.

Traditional musical instruments, known as *Tabla, Dhol, Dholok,* of drums and percussion group. The profession of making musical instruments continue through generations.

Top (right) : A potter is giving shape to his creation

Repairing a country-boat on a riverbank.
Boats play a major role in river transportation.

Dholok Badok - drummers, entertain people in village-fairs while they earn their livelihood by it

Buffalo and bullock carts play a vital role in rural transportation

A view of a roadside market

Pahela Boishakh, first day of Bengali New Year on 14 April, is celebrated with great fanfare. Colourful rallies are brought out to welcome the day.

Garlands of marigold placed on the wayside for sale

A smiling tribal beauty in traditional costume and make-up

Festival is an integral part of tribal life. A group of *Mro* community celebrating a festival.

Women at work in a leather factory.
Leather products of Bangladesh are
in high demand in the European market.

Glittering tomatoes heading for the market

A fleet of boats of *Bede*, a nomadic class who live in their boats and keep moving from one place to another. Professionally they are snake charmers. They also sell bangles, talisman etc.

Smiling gold, holding golden paddy

An *Iftar* market with traditional food items. Muslims take
Iftar to break fasting, which is observed from pre-dawn to dusk
in the month of Ramadan, the ninth month of Arabic calendar.

A woman doing needle–work at leisure time

Top (left) : The passing out parade of women cadet officers. Women are now increasingly adapting themselves to the changing needs of time and working shoulder to shoulder with men in fields, factories, offices and armed forces.

A smart march past of the women members of Bangladesh Ansar and Village Defence Party (VDP) during national day celebrations. VDP constitutes an auxiliary force.

A football match in progress

Top (right) : Fixing a target.
Women players at a billiard table.

Cricket has recently surpassed the popularity of
football. Bangladesh enjoys test status in cricket.

Eid congregation in the *Baitul Mukarram,*
the National Mosque of Bangladesh

Worshipping the goddess *Durga*
in a Hindu Temple

Decorating Christmas tree on the eve of Christmas

Top (right) : Traditional dance is a common feature
of religious rites of the tribe *'Rakhaine'*

Devotees at a Buddhist Pagoda

TRADITIONS

The indigenous customs and traditions which form the integral life cycle of the people have been nurtured through ages. Growing principally around agricultural practices, the main occupation of the people since the earliest settlement, traditional anniversaries include *Nabanna*, the festival of the new harvest and *Pahela Boishakh*, the Bangla New Year's day. Religion, particularly Islam, plays a dominant role in the life of the people and many of the rites, rituals and solemnities centre around religious beliefs like celebrations of the two *Eids*, *Ramadan* (the month of fasting), *Shab-e-Qadr* (the night of special significance), *Miladunnabi* (birth anniversary of the Prophet (SM), *Shab-e-Barat* (the night of fortune) etc. by the Muslim population; *Durga Puja* and *Kali Puja* (community worshipping of goddess *Durga* and *Kali*) by the Hindus, *Buddha Purnima* of the Buddhists and *Christmas* by the Christians. Participation by all communities in each other's religious ceremony is an indication of the long tradition of religious tolerance and harmony. Social customs like marriage, birth of a child, naming ceremony, funeral rites etc. have a distinct local flavour. National anniversaries include the Independence and National Day, the Victory Day and the historic Language Martyrs' Day, when the entire population join the celebrations with great enthusiasm and fervour.

Bangladesh is called a land of fairs and festivals. *Ekushey* Book Fair, Fair of *Muharram*, *Boishakhee* Mela, *Poush* Mela (Winter fair) and a number of tribal festivals are observed throughout the year. Many of these festivals continue for weeks together.

A doll in a bridal dress

81

A popular part of Spring Festival or *Basanta Utsav*; girls decorating each other with flower garlands

A rally in celebration of Bengali New Year's Day

Top (right) : Both young and old enjoying
a ride in the ferris wheel

Celebrating *Basanta Utsav* or Spring Festival;
women dressed in yellow tying
up bands of friendship

The Bengali New Year (14 April) begins with a traditional musical soiree at dawn in the capital Dhaka

A procession of foreign nationals on Dhaka streets on 21 February, the International Mother Language Day, to pay tributes to language martyrs

Beautiful pieces of clay pottery from Bangladesh.
The age-old tradition of pottery is getting
enriched with newer looks and designs.

A dance sequence in celebrating
Poush Mela (winter festival)

Bull fight is occasionally arranged in rural areas for mass entertainment

Traditional boat race - a favourite pastime during rainy season when rivers are full to the brim

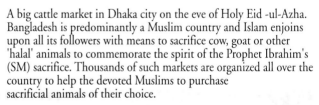

A big cattle market in Dhaka city on the eve of Holy Eid -ul-Azha. Bangladesh is predominantly a Muslim country and Islam enjoins upon all its followers with means to sacrifice cow, goat or other 'halal' animals to commemorate the spirit of the Prophet Ibrahim's (SM) sacrifice. Thousands of such markets are organized all over the country to help the devoted Muslims to purchase sacrificial animals of their choice.

Bauls (mystic singers) with their single-stringed musical instrument known as 'ektara' and 'tabor' tied to their waste, performing on the stage. *Baul* songs have a rich past and occupy an important place in the country's cultural arena.

Exquisite craftsmanship makes Bangladeshi jewellery exceedingly appealing

Decorating hands with henna, a reddish brown dye obtained from tropical plant, a popular custom among females and children; usually done during Eid festivals and marriage ceremonies

Women decorate their feet with *'alta'* (lac dye) on festive occasions

A bride in her majestic bridal attire

Top (left) : Traditional Palanquin has become rare with the advent of modern communication facilities. It is still found in remote localities.

A craftsman doing intricate needle–work on *katan sari*. It is a traditional outfit worn by women for their wedding.

Two boys in traditional Eid dress

Jamdani - the famed fabric of Bangladesh is admired for its fine texture, intricate design and quality yarns. *Jamdani sari* is a favourite lady's wear in many Asian countries.

Such an array of delicious sweetmeats
surely makes it hard to resist temptation

Pitha - homemade cake. Rice powder, molassses and coconut are its essential ingredients; it has a great tradition in rural Bangladesh.
Winter sees a great variety of this delicacy. *Pitha* festivals are held during this season.

Dhaka Rickshaws attract onlookers for their paintings,
whichs commonly display a collage of dazzling colours
and interesting subjects. A particular band of self-trained
painters are engaged in the profession of Rickshaw painting.

Top (right) : Glass bangles are still women's favourite
who like to have them glitter and jingle on their hands

Sheetal pati- a mat made of an indigenous plant,
is famous for its natural cooling effect. Colourfully
woven *Sheetal pati* displays a craftsmanship that
enrich the folk culture of the country.

A woman stitching *hatpakha*, a hand-fan,
to combat the hot days of summer

Top (right) : Traditional way of
spinning spindle for weaving cloth

A riverside market of clay pottery

Environment-friendly jute handicrafts
are in great demand both within and
outside Bangladesh

Top (right) : A woman potter is engaged
in decorating her products

The typical country boat made of palm
tree finds greater use during flood

A goldsmith deeply engrossed in his subtle work of art. Bangladesh enjoys widespread and longstanding reputation in filigree and jewellery.

Making conch bracelets. Crafts and ornaments made from conch shells occupy a notable place in the country's small and cottage industries.

Brassware has its distinct tradition

Blacksmiths are still surviving in
their profession. They make household
utensils and agricultural instruments.

97

'Bathing' – a water colour by Zainul Abedin (1914-1976), the pioneer of modern painting in Bangladesh and founder of the Institute of Fine Arts in Dhaka

ART AND CULTURE

Bangladesh is literally a multi-faceted cultural collage. Its deep-rooted heritage is amply reflected in its architecture, literature, dance, drama, music and painting. Influenced by three great religions—Hinduism, Buddhism and Islam in successive order, with Islam having the most pervading and lasting impact, Bangladesh has been a melting pot of diverse races and confluence of civilizations. Like a colourful montage, the cultural tradition of the country is a happy blending of many variants, unique in diversity but in essence largely symmetrical.

Specimens of ancient terracotta and pottery are glowing testimony to the rich tradition of art in Bangladesh. Sculpture, tapestry, engravings have developed alongside the mainstream contemporary art. Drama, mainly of indigenous origin, has a distinct flavour. Pantomime, puppet theatre, caricature, acrobatics and circuses have their own novelties. Architecture is a substantial reflection of the country's varied history. Music in Bangladesh has developed through centuries along three mainstreams—folk, modern and classical. Folk, tribal and classical are the prominent forms of dance along with middle-eastern variety. *Monipuri* and *Santal* dance have their own speciality and originality.

The earliest available specimen of Bangla literature is about one thousand years' old. Contemporary literature is a deep, prolific and pulsating process experimenting with social and critical realism. Articulate and animated production of films in recent years have brought for Bangladesh international accolades. Tribal culture is rich and varied and is a vital component of greater national culture. With the melange of forms, variations and creativity, Bangladesh's art and culture occupy a unique position—the people being their proud possessors.

A budding painter takes part in an art competition

'Naiyor' by Quamrul Hasan (1921-1988), a celebrated folk- based artist of the country

'Rural setting'—an oil painting by S M Sultan (1923-1994), distinguished for his bold and muscular human motif on a large canvas

Kazi Nazrul Islam (1898-1976), National Poet of Bangladesh. He is adored as the rebel poet for his bold anti-colonial role during the British period. Nazrul Islam was a pioneer of Islamic resurgence and his writings were a source of inspiration during the liberation war of Bangladesh in 1971.

Top right & below : Murals on folk motif

Bangla calligraphy based on Islamic ideology

Nakshikantha– occupies a distinct place in folk culture

A sequence from a contemporary dance composition

Traditional *Monipuri* Tribal dance. *Monipuris* live largely along the hilly frontiers of Sylhet district.

The shrine of 19th century mystic poet
Lalon Shah in Kushtia district. Every year
a *Baul* (mystic singer) festival is held at the
shrine site to mark his death anniversary.

Top (right) : Commemorative postal stamp
issued by Bangladesh Postal Department to
mark the death centenary of Lalon Shah

A *Baul* with his single-stringed musical instrument,
Ektara. *Baul* songs have a rich past and occupy an
important place in the country's indigenous culture.

106

Sequence of a tribal dance. Bangladesh has about two million tribal people mostly living in the hill districts. Better known are *Chakma, Marma,Lusai,Tipra,Murang, Punkho, Chak, Khumi, Riang, Mro, Kyang, Rakhain, Santal, Garo, Hajang, Bom, Tanchonga.* They are noted for their craftsmanship in weaving cloth and making ornaments and handicrafts.

Below : A scene from a modern drama, which received a spurt in recent times and attracted a new urban audience

Classical form of dance in Bangladesh occupies a dominant position. Folk, tribal and Middle-Eastern traits of dances are also popular.

DHAKA
THE CAPITAL CITY

Dhaka, the sprawling and bustling national metropolis of Bangladesh, has an exciting history and rich cultural heritage. Founded in 1608, the city alternately enjoyed the glory of being the capital of this part when it was successively under the Mughal, British and Pakistani rules. Standing on the bank of the river Buriganga, Dhaka became the capital of Bangladesh after it emerged as an independent and sovereign state in 1971. Once known as a city of 52 bazars and 53 lanes, Dhaka has a happy blend of Mughal, Victorian and modern architecture as well as a number of historical relics. The recent spurt in high–rise buildings is fast changing Dhaka's skyline. The city still has a name for its exotic culinary and cuisine and was once known world over as a *City of Mosques and Muslin*.

Nearby is *Sonargaon*, the old capital and throbbing river port of Narayanganj—the main trading point mostly dealing with jute having a cluster of jute mills. With its spacious national museum, lush green parks and zoo, serpentine lakes, tree-lining streets, open air bazars and colourful modern shopping plazas laden with traditional handicrafts and other items, posh and modern luxury hotels, Dhaka displays the exotic beauty of an enchanting oriental capital city. Art and artifacts, theatres, dance, drama and music having inimitable local touch flourish in Dhaka making it the country's prime cultural hub.

Dhaka's major waterfront *Sadarghat*, crowded with all kinds of rivercrafts, stands on the bank of the river *Buriganga*. Dhaka is also the hub of industrial, commercial and political activities of the country.

Dhaka Gate–the gateway from Zia International Airport to the metropolis

Sadarghat–Dhaka's main waterfront on the bank of the river *Buriganga*. Bangladesh is a riverine country where inland water transportation plays an important role in ferrying passengers and carrying goods. *Sadarghat* connects the outlying districts with the capital city through waterways.

Terminal building of Zia
International Airport

Partial view of Kamalapur Railway Station,
Dhaka. Railway is a vital sector in the
country's communication network.

Many airlines operate in Dhaka connecting Bangladesh to major cities of the world

Arrival Hall of Zia International Airport

Balaka, the impressive head office building of Biman Bangladesh Airlines

Summer blooms with red
Krishnachura along the
Crescent Lake

115

Majestic reflection of the
Jatiya Sangsad Bhaban on the
calm waters of surrounding lake

Session Hall of the
Jatiya Sangsad

Left : An aerial view of
Jatiya Sangsad Bhaban,
the National Parliament
complex at Sher-e-Bangla
Nagar in the capital city.
It is one of the rare
architectural edifices
created by world famous
architect Louis I. Kahn.

117

Bangabhaban–Office and Residence of the President

Office of the Prime Minister

The Supreme Court of Bangladesh. Judiciary in Bangladesh is monolithic in structure. The Chief Justice heads the Supreme Court. It consists of Appellate Division and High Court Division. The President appoints the Chief Justice and other Judges from among the advocates and members of the judicial service.

Top (left) : Main office of *Rajuk –Rajdhani Unnayan Kartripakkha* , the authority for expansion and development of the Capital city

A partial view of Bangladesh University of Engineering and Technology (BUET), Dhaka, which offers higher education in engineering and technology leading to Masters and Ph. D Programmes

TSC –Teachers-Students' Centre of Dhaka University, is the hub of extracurricular activities

Top (right) : Bangladesh-China Friendship Conference Centre – a modern centre for holding international conferences, built in Dhaka with financial and technical assistance of the People's Republic of China

Top view of Osmani Memorial Hall, Dhaka, built in memory of General M A G Osmani-Commander-in-Chief of Bangladesh Forces during the Liberation War in 1971

A view of the National
Stadium in Dhaka

Dhaka has turned
into a megacity

Fast changing skyline of Dhaka city

Inscription and decoration on the Mihrab of the Star
Mosque of old Dhaka, built in the 18th Century

A view of Gulshan
Mosque, noted for
its modern design.
Dotted with minarets
and domes, Dhaka is
literally a city of
mosques, many of
which were built
during the Mughal era.

Dhaka Shishu Park (Children's Park),
a place of fun for children

National Museum
at Shahbag, Dhaka

Below : Historic relics, paintings and other
collections preserved in the National Museum
reflect the heritage of the country

Ahsan Manzil—magnificent palace of the Nawabs of Dhaka on the bank of the river Buriganga. Built in the style of French architectural design, it has now been turned into a museum that displays the memorabilia of Nawab family.

Dhaka Sheraton Hotel complex, one of the modern hotels in Dhaka

A view of *Lalbagh Fort* in Dhaka, built in the early 18th century by the Mughal rulers. It has a distinct architectural design of the Mughal period. Adjacent to the fort is the tomb of *Poribibi,* daughter of Shaesta Khan, the Mughal Governor; it is admired widely for its superb interior decoration and the use of marble and streak-plates.

Karwan Bazar's SAARC Fountain at night

An inside view of the Pan Pacific Sonargaon Hotel

Top (left) : *Nagar Bhaban,* main office of Dhaka City Corporation. The grandeur of its architectural design attracts onlookers to behold its unique exterior look.

Top (middle) : The tranquil Dhanmondi lake bustles with visitors in the evenings

Top (right) : Kurmitola Golf Course, one of the famous golf resorts in the region

Below (left) : Office Building of the Ministry of Foreign affairs

Ashulia is an attractive holiday spot for city dwellers who care for leisure

One of the modern
Shopping Plazas in the Metropolis

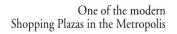

NATURE AND ITS RESOURCES

Bangladesh is literally a treasure-trove of rich and variegated natural beauty interspersed with enchanting landscape, mighty meandering rivers, exotic flora and fauna, picturesque resorts, long sunny beaches, tropical mangrove forests, fascinating art and architecture, ancient relics and archaeological sites and colourful tribal life. As a vacation land, Bangladesh has many facets. History and legends are intimately interwoven with the landmass together with the distinct traditions and cultural traits.

A familiar scene in a tea garden—returning to the factory with loads of tea leaves, forming a tapestry in white against the green background

131

Rafts of floating bamboo carried through the river. Bamboo, an essential item in daily life, has diverse usage in household activities, cottage industries, construction works and house-building.

Golpata grows abundantly along the creeks of Sundarbans. *Golpata* is used for making huts in the southern region of the country.

Bangladesh has considerable resources to augment its economic growth for providing a better living to its people. History records that till the advent of the British in the eighteenth century, Bangladesh had an enviable position in the entire region and was known as the legendary land of affluence and prosperity. The country has now almost achieved a green revolution. Diversified use of jute can restore for Bangladesh its past glory in the bulk production of the crop. Other crops such as rice, wheat, lentil, tea, sugarcane etc. are also cultivated on a large scale. Sub-sectors like fishery, livestock rearing, poultry and forestry are growing by leaps and bounds. The Bay of Bengal is literally a treasure–trove of sea fish and other wealth. Bangladesh's major natural resource is gas. There is also bright prospect of striking oil. Huge deposits of coal, limestone, peat, bitumin, hardrock, lignites, white clay etc. have already been identified and projects are being implemented for their harnessing for productive use.

The dense green Sundarbans, home of the Royal Bengal Tiger, declared as a world heritage site by UNESCO. Spotted deer, crocodile, monkey, python, wild boar and different species of birds fare prominently in its repertoire of wildlife.

Amidst a splendid panorama, Jafflong, a border outpost in Sylhet district is a scenic location with rare beauty of rolling stones from the hills, terraced tea gardens, flowing shallow rivulet and streams and tribal culture of *Khasia* origin.

A cotton field in full bloom. Two varieties of cotton are produced in Bangladesh– *shimul* and *karpas.*

134

A rice field extending up to the horizon. Rice is the staple food and the country's major crop. Bangladesh produces and exports fine quality rice.

Wheat cultivation is getting popular in the country

Sugarcane is grown abundantly in the country for manufacturing sugar and molasses

Maize is cultivated in some areas. Maize plant is also used as fodder.

Bangladesh has also many other valuable mineral resources. The best resources of the country are, however, its hardworking, devoted and dedicated citizens. It has all the ingredients and factors for a swift economic breakthrough.

Bangladesh has attracted travellers and tourists from far and near since the ancient times. They came all the way from Africa, Europe, Arabia, China and other regions. Some of them in their travelogues and memorabilia were quite effusive about the flourishing prosperity and bounty of nature in what is now Bangladesh.

137

Peeling off jute fibres from the jute plants.
Harvesting of jute plants and collection of
fibres take place in the rainy season.
Peeled off jute plants are used for various
purposes including manufacture of papers.

Traditional way of drying jute in the sun

A bee–hive hanging from a tree

Top (left) : Betel leaf cultivation. Chewing betel leaf with betel nut and lime is a popular habit of many people in the country. Bangladesh exports betel leaf to Middle-Eastern countries.

A rural jute purchasing centre vibrant with buyers and sellers. Bangladesh is the largest producer of jute.

Fishing in the tranquil Naaf river at Teknaf,
a border town with enchanting surroundings
of hills and ridges

Fishing in the Bay of Bengal,
a vast reservoir of sea-fishes
and other resources

140

Bangladesh exports both fresh and dry fish. Sea fishes are dried up in the sun while processing for export.

Pabda, an indigenous variety of fish known for its taste, especially in winter

In recent times, with the gradual development of infrastructure facilities and increasing exposition and openness, Bangladesh is fast emerging as an alluring tourist spot on the world map.

Bangladesh can be discovered and rediscovered by travelling through its chequered history and by experiencing the ecstasy of being in a land bedecked with serene natural beauty on a wide canvas of green.

Hilsa, distinctly a Bangladeshi fish, noted for its extraordinary flavour and taste

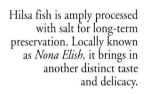

Hilsa fish is amply processed with salt for long-term preservation. Locally known as *Nona Elish,* it brings in another distinct taste and delicacy.

A wholesale fish market with large catches and crowds of buyers

143

Shrimps of Bangladesh are known worldwide for their quality and variety

A farmer is engaged in production of salt in the Cox's Bazar area. Traditionally salt is produced in the country by drying up the salty water of Bay of Bengal.

144

A canal of the Sundarbans during low tide. The deltaic swamps of Sundarbans are criss-crossed by rivers, canals and creeks.

The Foy's Lake in Chittagong with its idyllic setting

A picturesque landscape along the sea-beach of Cox's Bazar, an ideal resort for holidaying

A waterfall at Shubhalang in Rangamati hill district, which is known for its winding hills and enchanting beauty as well as colourful tribal culture

Sitakunda eco-park near Chittagong town, an attractive tourist spot well-known for its scenic setting in the tropical forest

The suspension bridge over the Kaptai lake, adjacent to Rangamati town

147

St. Martin's—the lone coral island in the Bay of Bengal off the coast of Chittagong. A popular vacation-land for both local and foreign tourists; its charm lies in its mystic and magical environment on the vast expanse of the blue sea.

Cox's Bazar beach, the longest and the natural in the world attracts tourist from across the countries

Boats and trawlers are used for fishing in the bay

149

Reflection of white clouds over the blue water of Kaptai lake, which flows across the hills and ridges displaying a unique beauty and tranquillity of nature

Fleet of fishing boats engaged in
catching fish in the bay near
St. Martin's Island

Wild flowers add to the captivating
beauty of the sandy sea–beach
at Cox's Bazar

Kuakata–a virgin sea-beach in southern Bangladesh

An enchanting view of sun–set on
the coral island of St. Martin's

Left : Handicrafts made from sea–shells
and corals are abundantly found
in sea-beaches

Hide and seek of light and shade
in the rainy season

Below (right) : White sea gulls sparkle in
the wind while flying across the blue sky,
forming a soothing contrast

The leisurely deer grazing amid graceful co-existence until there appears the king of the forest–tiger

An orchestra of flying birds soaring with
grace forming a part of the panorama of the sky

Top (left) : A gas field. Gas is the major natural resource of the country used for power generation, urea fertilizer production and domestic use.

Top (right) : Karnaphuli Fertilizer Company (KAFCO)–a Japan-Bangladesh joint-venture gas-based fertilizer factory in Chittagong.

Barapukuria coal mine in Dinajpur district. The estimated total deposit of high bituminous coal in the Barapukuria mine is 303 million tons.

Sunset at Kuakata sea–beach. The beach has its very own majestic
splendour–both sunrise and sunset can be viewed from here !

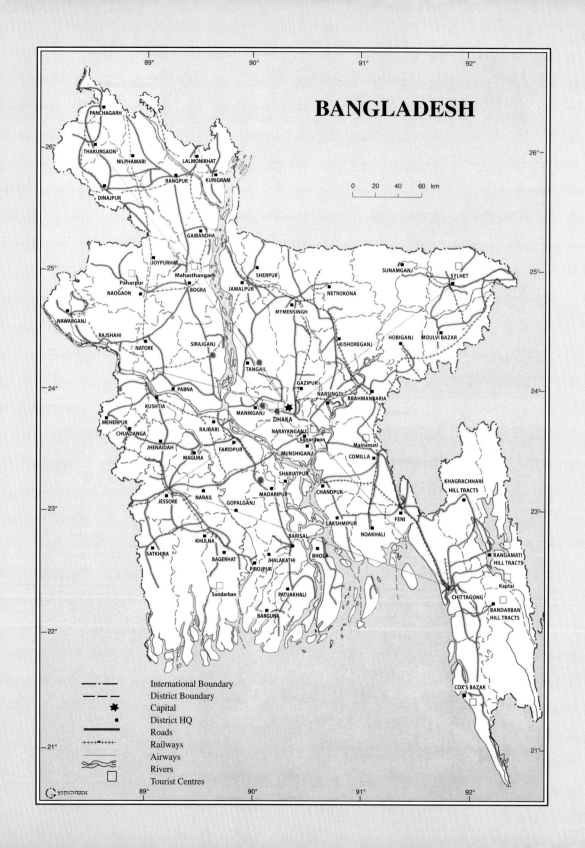

BANGLADESH

0 20 40 60 km

PANCHAGARH
THAKURGAON
NILPHAMARI   LALMONIRHAT
RANGPUR   KURIGRAM
DINAJPUR
GAIBANDHA
JOYPURHAT
Paharpur   Mahasthangarh   SHERPUR   SUNAMGANJ   SYLHET
NAOGAON   BOGRA   JAMALPUR   NETROKONA
NAWABGANJ   MYMENSINGH
RAJSHAHI   HOBIGANJ   MOULVI BAZAR
NATORE   SIRAJGANJ   KISHOREGANJ
                        TANGAIL
                                    GAZIPUR
PABNA   NARSINGDI   BRAHMANBARIA
KUSHTIA   MANIKGANJ   DHAKA
MEHERPUR   NARAYANGANJ
CHUADANGA   RAJBARI   Sonargaon   Mainamati
JHENAIDAH   FARIDPUR   MUNSHIGANJ   COMILLA
MAGURA   SHARIATPUR
                                                                KHAGRACHHARI
                        MADARIPUR   CHANDPUR   HILL TRACTS
JESSORE   NARAIL   GOPALGANJ
                                    LAKSHMIPUR   FENI
                        BARISAL   NOAKHALI
KHULNA   RANGAMATI
                                    BHOLA   HILL TRACTS
SATKHIRA   BAGERHAT   JHALAKATHI   Kaptai
                PIROJPUR
                                                        CHITTAGONG
Sundarban   PATUAKHALI   BANDARBAN
                BARGUNA   HILL TRACTS

                                                        COX'S BAZAR

— · — · —	International Boundary
— — —	District Boundary
★	Capital
▪	District HQ
———	Roads
+++++++	Railways
———	Airways
∿∿∿	Rivers
▫	Tourist Centres

COUNTRY PROFILE

The Country : The People's Republic of Bangladesh

Geographical Location : In South Asia; Location Between 20°34' and 26°38' north latitude and between 88°01' and 92°41' east longitude; consists of flat fertile alluvial land

Boundaries : North-India (Assam and Meghalaya), West-India (West Bengal), East-India (Tripura, Mizoram and Assam) and Myanmar, South-Bay of Bengal

Area : 1,47,570 square km. Territorial waters-12 nautical miles.

Capital City : Dhaka

Standard Time : GMT plus 6 hours

Climate : Sub-tropical monsoon

Average Temperature : Winter temperature (Nov-Feb) Maximum 29°C, Minimum 9°C. Summer temperature (Apr-Sep) Maximum 34°C, Minimum 21°C

Rainfall : 120-345 cm (47"-136") (Average during the Monsoon)

Humidity : Highest-99 percent (July) Lowest-36 percent (Dec)

Food : Staple diet rice, vegetable, pulses and fish

Principal Crops : Rice, Wheat, Jute, Tea, Tobacco and Sugarcane

Principal Rivers : Ganges/Padma, Brahmaputra/Jamuna, Meghna, Karnaphuli, Teesta etc. (total 230 rivers including tributaries)

Mineral Resources : Natural gas, limestone, hard rock, coal, lignite, silica sand, white clay, radioactive sand etc. (There is a strong possibility of oil deposits)

Human Resources : A substantial manpower reserve–well-trained and skilled engineers, economists, technicians, physicians, accountants and other professionals; trained administrative and managerial personnel; abundant, cheap, easily trained and adaptable, hardworking, intelligent and youthful labour force; labour rates between 1.5-2.0 US $/day

Foreign Trade : Total export earning during 2002-03 was US$ 6.55 billion. The principal exportables are ready-made garments, knitwear, frozen food, jute products, leather, chemical products and raw jute. Import payment during 2002-03 was US$ 9.09 billion.

Vegetation : Grassland, mixed evergreen and evergreen

Population : 133.4 million. Density—around 900 persons per sq. km

Literacy rate : 65 percent

Ethnic groups : Predominantly mixed groups of Proto-Australoids/Dravidians, Mongoloids and Aryans

Language : 99 percent Bangla, 1 percent other dialects. English is widely spoken and understood.

Religion : Muslim (88.3 percent), Hindu (10.5 percent), Buddhist (0.6 percent), Christian (0.3 percent) and Animists and believers in tribal faiths (0.1 percent)

History : Recorded history traceable to the fourth century B.C., with clear evidence of a flourishing civilization consisting of cities, places, temples, forts, seats of learning and monasteries; advent of the Muslim conquerors in 13th century AD; enjoying periods of prosperity under Muslim rule; seventeenth century–a time of economic wellbeing; 1757 : beginning of British colonial rule; 1947 : departure of the British from the Indian subcontinent; Bangladesh becomes "East Pakistan" as part of Pakistan; 1971 : emergence of the sovereign state of Bangladesh through an armed struggle for freedom

Sources : Bangladesh Bureau of Statistics (BBS), Export Promotion Bureau (EPB)

Design Director
K. G. Mustafa

Production Co-ordinator
Muhammad Mustafa

Map
Graphosman, Dhaka

Computer Graphics
Md. Mizanur Rahman
Power Print Limited

Photograph of the Prime Minister
Md. Lutfar Rahman Binu

Ptinted at
Zenith Packages Limited

Photographers

Abdul Malek Babul	Dr. Rashidun Nabi	Minhaj Mustakim	Saemul Haque
Abir Abdullah	Fazlur Rehman Jhinu	Md. Rizwanul Huda Raju	Shafiqul Alam Kiron/Map
ABM Siddique	Farhad Mahmud	Md. Shahidullah Kaiser	Shehab Uddin
Azizur Rahman	GMB Akash/Drik	M.Yousuf Tushar	Sohel Rana Ripon
Altaf Hossain	Jalal Uddin Haider	Mohammad Younus	Swapan Saha
ATM Monemul Haque	Kazi Akhtaruzzaman Nowab	Monowar Ahmed	Syed Zakir Hossain
Bayazid Akter	Mahmud/Map	Mufti Munir	Tahmid Mustafa
Bijon Sarkar	M.A Rahim	Nasir Mahmud	Tahmina Islam
Bikas Chandra Dey	Md. Harun-ur-Rashid	Nuruddin Ahmed	
Debaprasad das/Drik	Md. Mainuddin/Drik	Pankaj Sikder	
Dr. Noajesh Ahmed	Md. Monower Hussain Parvez	Rafiqul Islam/Prism	